BASIC COOKING

Galley Press

TABLE
OF
CONTENTS

APPETISERS
AND
SOUPS

Vichyssoise (page 6)

Vichyssoise

1 pound potatoes, pared and diced
1 large leek, sliced
3/4 pint chicken stock
Scant 1/2 pint milk

1 teaspoon salt
Pinch white pepper
Scant 1/2 pint single cream
Chopped chives

Place potatoes and leek in liquidiser or food processor; process until chopped. Place in saucepot; add enough water to cover. Cook until potatoes are tender. Drain. Put stock, milk, salt, and pepper into liquidiser or food processor. Add potato-leek mixture and process until smooth. Pour into bowls and stir in cream. Chill thoroughly before serving. Garnish with chopped chives.

Antipasto Appetiser Tray

1 packet (8 ounces) frozen asparagus,
    cooked according to directions
1 packet (8 ounces) frozen cauliflower,
    partially cooked
1 jar (8 ounces) stoned olives, drained
1 cucumber, thinly sliced
4 firm tomatoes, cut into thin wedges
8 ounces mushrooms, sliced

8 fluid ounces French dressing
4 ounces salami
4 ounces smoked ham or tongue
6 ounces sliced Gruyère cheese, cut into
    quarters
Lettuce leaves
Carrot strips

Place vegetables in separate containers; pour dressing over vegetables. Cover; marinate in refrigerator overnight. Drain. Arrange vegetables, meats, and cheese on lettuce-covered platter. Garnish with carrot strips.

Antipasto Appetiser Tray
From the Quick and Easy Armour Cookbook Copyright 1980 by Armour and Company.

Bacon-Mushroom Crowns

40 appetisers

40 medium-size mushrooms
8 rashers streaky bacon, derinded, diced, and crisply cooked
4 ounces grated mild Cheddar or Chesire cheese
4 ounces butter or margarine, softened

2 ounces fine breadcrumbs
2 cloves garlic, crushed
1 small onion, finely chopped
1 tablespoon dry red wine
1/2 teaspoon salt

Remove and chop stems from cleaned mushrooms; combine stems with remaining ingredients. Fill mushroom caps; place on grill, stuffing-side up. Grill 5 to 7 minutes, or until light brown and bubbly.

Prawn Pâté

About 1 pint

1/4 ounce unflavoured gelatine
3 1/2 tablespoons lemon juice
3/4 pint fresh sour cream
6 fluid ounces chilli sauce
2 tablespoons horseradish sauce

8 ounces prawns, cleaned, cooked, and finely chopped
Parsley (optional)
Green olives (optional)

In medium-size saucepot, mix gelatine with lemon juice and 1 tablespoon water; leave 1 minute. Stir over moderate heat until gelatine is completely dissolved, about 1 minute. Remove from heat; cool. Blend in sour cream, chilli sauce, and horseradish; fold in prawns. Turn into 1 1/2-pint mould; chill until firm. Unmould onto serving plate. Garnish with parsley and green olives.

Chicken Liver Pâté

1/2 pint

8 ounces chicken livers
2 ounces butter or margarine
1 medium-size onion, sliced
2 hard-boiled eggs

1/4 teaspoon salt
1/8 teaspoon pepper
1/8 teaspoon thyme

Cut livers in half; remove membranes. Heat fat in frying pan. Add livers and onion; fry over moderate heat, stirring occasionally, until livers are brown and onion is transparent. Put 1 egg into liquidiser or food processor; process until chopped. Repeat with second egg. Add half the liver-onion mixture together with salt, pepper, and thyme; process until chopped. Add remaining liver mixture; process until smooth. Turn into serving dish and chill.

Prawn Pâté

Old-Fashioned Mushroom Soup 8 servings

8 ounces mushrooms
3 ounces butter or margarine, divided
16 ounces carrots, finely chopped
4 celery sticks, finely chopped
2 medium-size onions, finely chopped
1 clove garlic, finely chopped
2 tins (10½ ounces each) condensed beef consommé or 1 pint beef stock
3 tablespoons tomato purée
¼ teaspoon salt
⅛ teaspoon pepper
4 parsley sprigs
Celery leaves
1 bay leaf
3 tablespoons dry sherry
Fresh sour cream

Finely chop half the mushrooms; slice remaining half and set aside. In large saucepot, melt 2 ounces fat. Add chopped mushrooms and sauté 5 minutes. Add carrots, celery, onions, and garlic; sauté 5 minutes longer. Combine consommé and enough water to make 1½ pints. Add to vegetables together with tomato purée, salt and pepper. Tie parsley, celery leaves, and bay leaf together; add to saucepot. Bring to the boil. Cover; reduce heat and simmer 1 hour. Remove parsley, celery leaves, and bay leaf and discard. Purée soup in liquidiser. Return to saucepot. In medium-size frying pan, melt 1 ounce fat. Add reserved sliced mushrooms and sauté 5 minutes. Add to soup along with sherry; reheat. Garnish with sour cream.

French Onion Soup About 8 servings

2 pounds onions
4 ounces butter or margarine
3 tins (10½ ounces each) beef consommé
2 tablespoons dry white wine
1 tablespoon Worcestershire sauce
1 French loaf
2 tablespoons grated Parmesan cheese
1 ounce Emmental cheese, grated
Butter

Peel and thinly slice onions. In large saucepot, melt fat and add onions; fry over low heat, stirring often, until soft and golden, about 30 minutes. Add consommé, 1 soup tin water, wine, and Worcestershire. Bring to the boil. Reduce heat and simmer, covered, 30 minutes. Preheat oven to 180°C. (350°F.), Gas Mark 4. Cut bread into 4-cm (1½-inch) slices; place on tin; toast in oven 20 minutes. Increase temperature to 200°C. (400°F.), Gas Mark 6. Pour soup into ovenproof casserole or tureen. Place toast on top of soup. Combine cheeses and sprinkle on top. Dot with additional butter. Place in oven until cheese is melted, about 5 to 8 minutes.

Parsley-Cheese Ball

One 7.5-cm (3-inch) ball

3 ounces cream cheese, softened
3 tablespoons dry sherry
1/2 teaspoon Worcestershire sauce
8 ounces mature Cheddar cheese, grated

Pinch onion salt
Pinch garlic salt or powder
Pinch celery salt
4 tablespoons chopped parsley

Beat cream cheese, sherry, and Worcestershire until smooth. Add Cheddar cheese and seasoned salt; beat until well mixed. Turn mixture onto aluminium foil or greaseproof paper and shape into ball. Refrigerate several hours or overnight. About 30 minutes before serving time, put parsley on greaseproof paper; roll cheese ball in parsley to coat completely. Refrigerate wrapped in plastic or waxed paper.

Cream of Spinach Soup

4 servings

1 ounce butter or margarine
1 small onion, chopped
1 packet (8 ounces) frozen chopped
spinach, thawed
1 tin (10 1/2 ounces) condensed chicken
broth

2 tablespoons plain flour
1/4 teaspoon salt or to taste
Pinch nutmeg
1/2 pint double cream
Watercress for garnish

Melt butter in saucepot. Add onion and cook until transparent. Add spinach and chicken broth; cover and cook 5 minutes. Pour into liquidiser and blend until smooth. Add flour, salt and nutmeg; blend mixture and return to saucepot. Cook over moderate heat, stirring occasionally, until thickened, about 5 minutes. Stir into cream. Heat but do not boil. Ladle into bowls. Garnish with watercress.

Gazpacho

3/4 pint tomato juice
1 clove garlic, halved
1 small onion, cut up
1/2 green pepper, cored, seeded and cut up
1 small cucumber, pared and cut up
2 ripe tomatoes, pared, cored, and
    cut up

3 tablespoons olive oil
3 tablespoons red wine vinegar
1 1/2 teaspoons salt
1/4 teaspoon pepper
    Garnish: chopped onion, green pepper,
       tomato, and cucumber (optional)

Put all ingredients except chopped-vegetable garnish into liquidiser or food processor in order listed. Cover; process until vegetables are finely chopped. Chill several hours or overnight. Garnish with chopped onion, green pepper, tomato, and cucumber.

Pumpkin Soup

3/4 pint chicken stock, divided
1/2 green pepper, cored, seeded and cut up
1 small onion, cut up
1 parsley sprig
1/4 teaspoon thyme
16 ounces cooked pumpkin

1 tablespoon plain flour
1 ounce butter or margarine
    Scant 1/2 pint milk
1 teaspoon castor sugar
1/2 teaspoon nutmeg
1/2 teaspoon salt

Put 1/2 pint stock, green pepper, onion, parsley, and thyme into liquidiser. Cover; blend until vegetables are coarsely chopped. Pour into saucepot; simmer 5 minutes. Return mixture to liquidiser; add pumpkin and flour. Cover; blend until smooth. Pour into saucepot; stir in remaining stock and remaining ingredients. Heat to boiling, stirring often; simmer 3 minutes.

Gazpacho

PLAIN AND FANCIFUL MAIN COURSES

Coq au Vin (page 17)

Coq au Vin

4 rashers streaky bacon, derinded and
    diced
4 ounces butter or margarine
2 grilling-frying chickens,
    (2½ to 3 pounds each),
    quartered
16 button onions
16 large mushrooms
2 cloves garlic, minced

1 bunch spring onions, sliced
1 ounce plain flour
1½ pints dry red wine
2 chicken stock cubes
2 teaspoons salt
¼ teaspoon pepper
½ teaspoon thyme
1 bay leaf

In large heavy casserole or saucepot, cook bacon over moderate heat until crisp; remove bacon pieces and reserve. Add fat to bacon drippings; add chicken pieces and brown on all sides. Remove chicken and reserve. Place onions and mushrooms in casserole and brown lightly; remove and reserve. Pour out all but 2 tablespoonfuls drippings. Add garlic and spring onions and cook until spring onions are soft. Add flour and cook 2 minutes, stirring constantly, until flour is browned. Remove from heat; add wine, stock cubes, and scant ½ pint boiling water. Return to heat and cook, stirring until mixture comes to the boil. Season with salt, pepper, thyme, and bay leaf. Add reserved bacon, chicken pieces, onions, and mushrooms. Reduce heat; cover tightly and simmer 30 to 45 minutes, or until chicken is tender. Remove bay leaf before serving.

Roast Beef in a Jacket

2 tablespoons vegetable oil
2 cloves garlic, finely chopped
2 teaspoons basil
1 beef sirloin joint (4 to 5 pounds),
    boned and rolled
    Pepper

3 ounces butter or margarine, melted
6 ounces fine breadcrumbs
6 tablespoons finely snipped parsley,
    divided
3 to 4 spring onions, finely chopped
    Paprika

Preheat oven to 240°C. (475°F.), Gas Mark 9. Combine oil, garlic, and basil; mix well. Brush beef on all sides with garlic mixture, covering well; sprinkle lightly with pepper. Place rack in roasting tin and meat on rack. Roast 30 minutes. Meanwhile, combine fat, crumbs, 4 tablespoons parsley, and spring onions, tossing lightly to mix well. Remove beef from oven. Working quickly, press crumb mixture on top, sides, and ends of beef. Sprinkle with paprika. Return beef to oven. For rare beef, roast 15 to 20 minutes longer, or until meat thermometer registers 125°F. (Add 10 minutes for medium-rare. Beyond that point, beef cooked in this manner will not be tender and juicy.) Remove from oven and leave 10 minutes. To serve, sprinkle with remaining parsley; cut into thin diagonal slices.

Roast Beef in a Jacket

Sukiyaki

4 to 6 servings

8 fluid ounces soy sauce
6½ tablespoons sake (rice wine) or dry
white wine
2½ tablespoons castor sugar
2 pounds beef sirloin, thinly sliced
Butter or margarine
Chinese noodles or dried noodles,
soaked
1 small tin bamboo shoots

4 bunches spring onions,
cut into 3.8-cm (1½-inch)
lengths
2 large onions, thinly sliced
Optional vegetables: fresh
mushrooms, celery, spinach,
watercress, bean sprouts, Chinese
cabbage, pea pods

Combine soy sauce, 8 fluid ounces water, sake, and sugar in jug and set aside. Arrange meat on 1 large or 2 medium-size trays or platters. Dot with fat. Drain Chinese noodles and bamboo shoots and place around meat. Arrange spring onions and onions on platter. Select 2 or 3 vegetables from list to add to platter. Mushrooms should be thinly sliced. Celery should be cleaned and cut on diagonal. Use small center leaves of spinach. Chinese cabbage should be cut into shreds. Remove tips and strings from pea pods. Prepare Sukiyaki at table in 2 separate cookings. Melt fat in frying pan. Add half the meat; quick-fry 1 minute. Add half the noodles, bamboo shoots, spring onions, and selected vegetables. Pour half the sauce mixture over top. Cook, uncovered, about 7 minutes or until crisp-tender, stirring lightly. Serve immediately. Continue with remaining meat and vegetables.

Swiss Steak

8 servings

8 rump joint steaks
3 ounces plain flour, divided
2 to 3 ounces fat or drippings
1 tablespoon salt
½ teaspoon savoury

¼ teaspoon pepper
2 tins (14 ounces each) tomatoes
2 celery sticks, chopped
1 small green pepper, cored, seeded,
and chopped

Coat steaks with 2 ounces flour. In large frying pan, heat shortening; add meat and brown well. Transfer steaks to large shallow baking tin. Preheat oven to 160°C. (325°F.), Gas Mark 3. Blend remaining flour and seasonings into pan drippings. Gradually stir in ¾ pint water, then add tomatoes, celery, and green pepper. Cook and stir until slightly thickened. Pour over meat; cover and bake about 2 hours, or until meat is tender.

Sukiyaki

Golden Mushroom Beef Tips

6 servings

2 pounds sirloin, cut into 2.5-cm (1-inch) cubes
2 ounces butter or margarine
3 fluid ounces dry sherry
1 clove garlic, minced

2 tins (10½ ounces each) cream of mushroom soup
1 tablespoon finely chopped onion
Cooked noodles

In frying pan, brown beef in fat. Add remaining ingredients and 8 fluid ounces water. Cover and cook over low heat, stirring occasionally, 2 hours or until tender. Serve over noodles.

Pastitsio

8 servings

1½ pounds minced beef
2 medium-size onions, chopped
6 tablespoons Hunt's tomato purée
2 teaspoons salt
½ teaspoon pepper
¼ teaspoon ground cinnamon
¼ teaspoon ground nutmeg

1 packet (7¼ ounces) macaroni and cheese dinner
¾ pint milk
3 eggs, slightly beaten
1½ ounces Parmesan cheese, grated
4 slices processed cheese, cut diagonally in half

In frying pan, brown beef and onion; drain fat. Stir in tomato purée, ⅔ pint water, salt, pepper, cinnamon, and nutmeg. Cover and simmer 10 minutes. Meanwhile, cook macaroni according to packet directions; drain. Mix contents of cheese sauce packet with milk in saucepot; cook over low heat, stirring until smooth. Add eggs; continue cooking and stirring until sauce is slightly thickened and creamy. Preheat oven to 160°C. (325°F.), Gas Mark 3. Place half the cooked macaroni in greased baking dish; cover with meat mixture. Sprinkle with Parmesan, then remaining macaroni. Pour cheese sauce over top. Bake 40 minutes, or until topping is set. Arrange processed cheese triangles on top, overlapping; bake about 2 minutes longer.

Golden Mushroom Beef Tips

Danish Pork Chops

4 servings

4 pork chops, cut 2 cm (¾ inch) thick
½ ounce butter or margarine
2 large apples, peeled, cored, and
    chopped

4 ounces prunes, finely chopped
¼ pint chicken stock
¼ pint double cream
    Salt and pepper

Trim as much fat as possible from pork chops. In heavy frying pan, melt fat. Add pork chops and brown lightly on both sides. Add apples, prunes, stock, and cream. Season lightly with salt and pepper. Cover and simmer 45 minutes, or until chops are tender. Stir sauce occasionally and, if sauce becomes too thick, add a little water. Remove chops. Skim off as much fat as possible from top of gravy and press through sieve. Heat thoroughly and serve with chops.

Beef Ragoût

7 servings

2 pounds stewing beef
2 celery sticks, cut into pieces
1 medium-size onion, cut into 8 pieces
2 medium-size carrots, halved and cut
    into slices
1 tin (14 ounces) tomatoes

6 ounces ready-cooked tapioca
1 tablespoon castor sugar
2½ teaspoons salt
½ teaspoon pepper
1 bay leaf

Preheat oven to 150°C. (300°F.), Gas Mark 2. Combine all ingredients in 1¾-pint casserole. Remove and discard bay leaf. Cover and bake 3 hours.

Pineapple-Rum Glazed Ham

18 to 20 servings

1 tin (5 pounds) ham
3 ounces soft brown sugar
4 ounces orange marmalade
1 tablespoon rum

1 tin (20 ounces) sliced pineapple,
    drained, 4 tablespoons juice
    reserved
    Whole cloves

Preheat oven to 160°C. (325°F.), Gas Mark 3. Place ham on rack in roasting tin and bake 1½ to 2 hours. Combine brown sugar, orange marmalade, rum and 4 tablespoons reserved pineapple juice. Cook over low heat, stirring until well blended. About 30 minutes before ham is done, remove from oven. Arrange pineapple slices over ham, attaching with whole cloves. Brush with marmalade mixture. Bake 30 minutes longer, spooning glaze over twice.

Danish Pork Chops

Ham Balls in Orange Sauce

6 to 8 servings

1 pound ham, minced
1/2 pound fresh pork, minced
2 ounces breadcrumbs
1 medium-size onion, chopped
1/2 teaspoon made mustard
1/4 pint milk

2 eggs
2 1/2 ounces dark brown sugar
1 tablespoon cornflour
1/4 teaspoon ground cloves
2/3 pint orange juice

Preheat oven to 180°C. (350°F.), Gas Mark 4. Combine ham, pork, crumbs, onion, mustard, milk, and eggs in large bowl; mix well. Form into 3.8-cm (1 1/2-inch) balls and place in pie plate. Bake 30 minutes. Meanwhile, combine brown sugar, cornflour, and cloves in saucepot; stir in orange juice. Cook over moderate heat, stirring constantly, until thickened. Reduce heat; keep sauce warm until ham balls are cooked. Drain ham balls on kitchen paper, then add to sauce in casserole. Cover; simmer 15 to 20 minutes, until both ham balls and sauce are hot.

Russian Stuffed Cabbage

4 to 6 servings

1 large cabbage
1/4 pound pork, minced
1 cup cooked long-grain rice
1 medium-size onion, finely chopped
Salt and pepper

1/4 pint beef stock
3 ounces raisins
1/4 pint orange juice
Boiled potatoes (optional)

Cut core from cabbage. Place cabbage in boiling water and boil until leaves separate without tearing. Select 8 to 12 large leaves; trim off midribs so leaves roll easily. Reserve remaining cabbage for later use. Combine pork, rice, and onion; add salt and pepper to taste. Divide mixture on cabbage leaves. Roll leaves firmly around mixture, tucking edges inside to contain stuffing. Secure tightly with wooden cocktail sticks or tie with thread. Arrange cabbage rolls close together in frying pan. Combine stock, raisins, and orange juice; pour over rolls. Cover and simmer over low heat 45 to 50 minutes, or until cabbage is tender and pork is cooked. Check occasionally and, if necessary, add more broth to keep cabbage from sticking to pan. Arrange cabbage rolls on heated platter. Serve with sauce from pan and plain boiled potatoes.

Ham Balls in Orange Sauce

Chicken with Pea Pods

8 servings

4 whole chicken breasts, skinned, boned, and halved
2½ teaspoons salt, divided
  Cooking oil
1 tin (20 ounces) pineapple chunks in unsweetened juice

2 tins (8 ounces each) water chestnuts, drained and thinly sliced
5 tablespoons black treacle
3½ tablespoons soy sauce
2 chicken stock cubes
8 ounces pea pods
1 tablespoon cornflour

Cut each breast half into 10 to 12 strips. Sprinkle strips with 2 teaspoons salt. Heat oil in frying pan over moderate-high heat; add chicken and cook, stirring constantly, about 3 minutes, or until chicken turns white. Drain pineapple, reserving chunks. Add pineapple juice, water chestnuts, treacle, soy sauce, ½ pint water, and stock cubes to chicken. Mix well. Reduce heat; cover and simmer 5 to 10 minutes, or until chicken is tender. Add reserved pineapple chunks, pea pods, and remaining ½ teaspoon salt. Cover and simmer 2 more minutes, stirring occasionally. Blend cornflour and 6½ tablespoons cold water to make smooth paste. Add to chicken mixture and cook, stirring, until sauce is clear and thickened.

Moussaka

6 servings

1 pound lamb or pork, minced
1 medium-size onion, chopped
4 tablespoons vegetable oil, divided
1 large aubergine
1 teaspoon salt
¼ teaspoon pepper
¼ teaspoon ground nutmeg

6 tablespoons Hunt's tomato purée
4 ounces mushrooms, sliced
½ ounce butter
1 ounce soft breadcrumbs
2 tablespoons grated Parmesan cheese
2 tablespoons chopped parsley

In large frying pan, sauté meat and onion in 2 tablespoons oil until onion is transparent. Peel aubergine and cut into cubes. Add to frying pan with 2 tablespoons remaining oil; toss to mix. Cook, stirring occasionally, 5 to 10 minutes, until aubergine is tender. Add salt, pepper, and nutmeg. Preheat oven to 200°C., (400°F.), Gas Mark 6. In 2-pint casserole, combine tomato purée, ¼ pint water, and mushrooms. Add aubergine mixture; mix thoroughly. In small frying pan, melt butter. Add breadcrumbs, Parmesan, and parsley; toss to mix. Sprinkle over casserole. Bake, uncovered, 15 to 20 minutes.

Chicken with Pea Pods

Liver and Tomatoes

2 rashers streaky bacon, derinded and halved
1 ounce plain flour
2 teaspoons salt, divided
1/4 teaspoon pepper

1 pound ox liver
1 medium-size onion, chopped
1 celery stick, diced
1 tin (14 ounces) tomatoes
1/2 teaspoon chilli powder

In large frying pan, fry bacon until crisp. Remove from pan; set aside. Combine flour, 1 teaspoon salt, and pepper. Remove heavy membranes and veins from liver and cut into strips. Coat with seasoned flour; brown with onion and celery in bacon drippings in frying pan. Add tomatoes, 1 teaspoon salt, and chilli powder. Cook, stirring occasionally, 10 minutes, or until liver is tender. Garnish with bacon.

Duckling à l'Orange

4 servings

1 duckling (4½ to 5 pounds)
1 tin (10½ ounces) beef consommé or ½ pint beef stock
Scant ½ pint orange juice
3 tablespoons Curaçao
1½ tablespoons cornflour

1 tablespoon honey
1 teaspoon lemon juice
1 tablespoon orange zest, cut into thin strips
Orange sections (optional)
Cherries (optional)

Prick duckling and place on rack in shallow baking tin. Roast at 160°C. (325°F.), Gas Mark 3, for 2 to 2 hours 30 minutes (about 30 minutes per pound). Meanwhile, in saucepot, combine remaining ingredients except orange zest, orange sections, and cherries. Cook sauce until thickened, stirring constantly. Remove duck from tin; pour off excess fat. Stir sauce into drippings in pan. Add orange zest; heat. Carve duckling and arrange on serving platter. Pour part of sauce over duckling; serve remaining sauce. Garnish with orange sections and cherries.

Duckling à l'Orange

Veal Birds

6 servings

6 veal steaks (1 1/2 pounds)
4 slices bread, divided
1 medium-size onion, cut up
1/2 teaspoon salt
1/4 teaspoon pepper
4 parsley sprigs

6 tablespoons butter or margarine,
   divided
1 tin (10 1/2 ounces) beef consommé or
   1/2 pint beef stock, divided
  Plain flour, divided
1/2 teaspoon thyme
1/2 teaspoon oregano

Beat veal to 6-mm (1/4-inch) thickness; set aside. Tear 2 slices bread and place in liquidiser or food processor; add onion. Cover; process until onion is chopped. Empty into bowl. Tear remaining 2 slices bread and place in liquidiser or food processor; add salt, pepper, and parsley. Cover; process until bread is crumbed. Add to onion mixture. Melt 3 tablespoons fat and stir in with 3 tablespoons consommé. Divide mixture evenly on veal steaks; roll up; secure with wooden cocktail sticks or clean string in several places. Roll in flour; shake off excess. Heat remaining 3 tablespoons fat in frying pan; brown birds well on all sides; remove; keep warm. Stir thyme, oregano, and 1 tablespoon flour into fat in frying pan. Add 1/4 pint water and remaining consommé. Stir to loosen brown bits on sides of pan; stir rapidly over moderate heat until thickened and bubbly. Return veal birds to frying pan. Cover; simmer over low heat 10 minutes. Remove cocktail sticks or snip string carefully from each veal bird.

Old-Fashioned Butter-Roasted Chicken

Rub skin of roasting chicken generously with softened fat. Place bird, breast-side up, on rack in shallow baking pan or open roaster. Cover with double thickness of cheesecloth dipped in melted fat. Roast according to timetable that follows. Baste often with pan drippings or more fat. The bird is done when the juices run yellow with no tinge of pink at the leg joint.

Chicken Roasting Timetable

READY-TO-COOK WEIGHT	TIME (APPROXIMATE)	OVEN TEMPERATURE
2 to 3 pounds	2 1/4 hours	160°C. (325°F.), Gas Mark 3
3 1/2 to 4 pounds	2 3/4 hours	160°C. (325°F.), Gas Mark 3
4 1/2 to 5 pounds	3 1/2 hours	160°C. (325°F.), Gas Mark 3

Old-Fashioned Butter-Roasted Chicken

Baked Chicken Parmesan

8 servings

6 slices bread, divided
2 tablespoons parsley sprigs
1½ ounces Parmesan cheese, grated
2 teaspoons salt
6 ounces butter or margarine, melted

1 clove garlic, crushed
2 teaspoons Dijon mustard
1 teaspoon Worcestershire sauce
2 grilling-frying chickens (2½ to 3 pounds each), cut up

Break 2 slices bread into liquidiser or food processor and process until crumbed. Empty into shallow pan. Repeat process with remaining bread, leaving crumbs from last 2 slices in container. Add parsley and process until chopped. Gradually add cheese, processing until grated. Add mixture to crumbs in shallow pan. Add salt; mix well. Preheat oven to 180°C. (350°F.), Gas Mark 4. Combine fat, garlic, mustard, and Worcestershire in bowl. Dip chicken pieces into fat mixture; roll in crumb-cheese mixture. Place pieces in single layer in large shallow baking tin. Bake about 1 hour, or until chicken is tender, basting occasionally with pan drippings.

Chicken Curry

6 servings

4 ounces desiccated coconut
¼ pint milk, scalded
1 medium-size onion, cut up
1 celery stick, cut up
1 cooking apple, pared, quartered, and cored
1 ounce butter or margarine
2 tablespoons plain flour
1 tablespoon mild curry powder

1 teaspoon salt
⅛ teaspoon pepper
½ teaspoon ginger
⅔ pint chicken stock, divided
1 pound cooked chicken, diced
1 tablespoon lemon juice
¼ pint double cream
Cooked rice (optional)
Condiments (optional)

Put coconut and scalded milk into liquidiser. Cover; blend until coconut is pulverized. Strain into small bowl through fine sieve or double-thick cheesecloth; set aside. Put onion, celery, and apple into liquidiser; add water just to cover; blend until vegetables and apple are chopped. Drain thoroughly in colander. Heat fat in large frying pan. Add onion, celery, and apple; cook over moderate heat, stirring occasionally, 5 minutes. Stir in flour, curry, salt, pepper, and ginger; cook over low heat, stirring constantly, 3 minutes. Put contents of frying pan and 6½ tablespoons chicken stock into liquidiser. Cover; blend until smooth. Return mixture to pan; add remaining chicken stock and coconut milk. Cook, stirring, until mixture comes to the boil. Cover; simmer over low heat 20 minutes. Add chicken and lemon juice; cook until thoroughly heated. Just before serving, stir in cream; heat gently. Serve over cooked rice and accompany with any of the following condiments: chutney, salted peanuts, banana slices, desiccated coconut, and sultanas.

Old-Fashioned Pot Roast

10 to 12 servings

1 ounce fat or vegetable oil
5 to 6 pounds beef silverside
   Salt and pepper, divided
1 tin (10½ ounces) beef consommé
   or ½ pint beef stock
1 tomato, cored and quartered
1 medium-size onion, cut up
1 clove garlic, halved

2 carrots, pared and cut up
1 celery stick with leaves, cut up
1 green pepper, cored, seeded and
   cut up
1 bay leaf
1 ounce plain flour (optional)
   Chopped parsley (optional)

In casserole or saucepot, heat fat; add beef and brown on all sides. Drain off fat. Season meat with 2 teaspoons salt and ¼ teaspoon pepper. Add consommé, vegetables, and bay leaf. Cover; cook over low heat about 3 hours, or until meat is tender, basting meat occasionally with pan juices. Remove meat; set aside. Skim fat from gravy and discard; remove and discard bay leaf. Put gravy with vegetables into liquidiser. If thicker gravy is desired, add 1 ounce flour. Cover; blend until smooth. Season to taste. Leave meat whole or slice; return meat and gravy to casserole to keep warm until serving time. Sprinkle with chopped parsley.

Chicken Fondue

4 servings

2 whole chicken breasts, skinned,
   boned, and halved
2½ ounces plain flour
1 egg, well beaten

4 ounces fine breadcrumbs
1¼ pints cooking oil
   Sour Cream-Apricot Sauce
   (recipe follows)

Cut each breast half into 2-cm (¾-inch) pieces. Coat pieces with flour, dip into egg, then coat lightly and evenly with breadcrumbs. In saucepot, heat oil. Pour into fondue pan and place directly over heat. Spear piece of chicken with fondue fork and hold in hot oil until golden brown. Remove from fondue fork to serving plate. Dip in Sour Cream-Apricot Sauce.

Sour Cream-Apricot Sauce

About 1¼ pints

½ pint fresh sour cream
1 jar (12 ounces) apricot jam

3 tablespoons Dijon mustard

In small bowl, combine all ingredients. Refrigerate to chill well before serving.

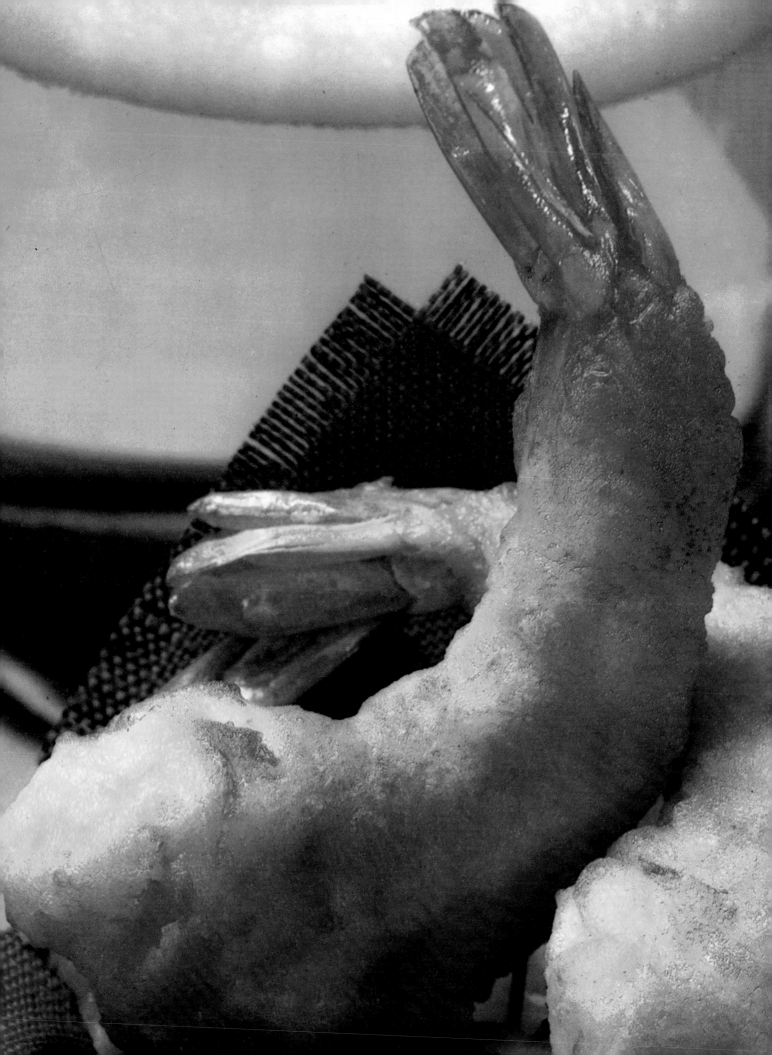

Batter-Fried Prawns

2 eggs
1/4 pint milk
4 ounces plain flour, stirred before measuring
1 teaspoon baking powder
1 teaspoon salt

2 teaspoons cooking oil
2 pounds fresh or thawed frozen whole prawns
Fat
Orange Sauce (recipe follows)
Plum Hot (recipe follows)

Whisk together eggs and milk until frothy. Sift together flour, baking powder, and salt. Add to egg mixture; add oil and beat until mixture is smooth and well blended. Set aside. Remove shells from prawns, leaving tails on. Make a shallow cut lengthways along outside curve. Lift out vein; wash prawns and flatten so they remain open. Drain well on kitchen paper. Pour enough fat to more than cover prawns into large frying pan. Heat over moderate heat. Dip prawns into batter, one at a time, and fry in batches about 4 minutes, or until golden brown and puffy. Drain on kitchen paper. Serve immediately with Orange Sauce or Plum Hot.

Orange Sauce   About ¾ pint

1 jar (12 ounces) orange marmalade
1 clove garlic

1 piece whole ginger root or 1/2 teaspoon ground ginger

In saucepot, combine all ingredients and cook over low heat, stirring constantly, until mixture bubbles. Remove garlic and ginger root.

Plum Hot   About ¾ pint

1 jar (12 ounces) plum jam
1 to 2 cloves garlic, very finely minced

2 teaspoons soy sauce
1/4 teaspoon pepper

In saucepot, combine all ingredients and cook over low heat, stirring occasionally, at least 5 minutes, or until garlic is cooked. Remove from heat and cool slightly.

Batter-Fried Prawns

Poached Salmon

8 fluid ounces dry white wine
1 tablespoon vinegar
1 carrot, sliced
1 large onion, sliced
1 celery stick and leaves, sliced
2 parsley sprigs

1 bay leaf
6 peppercorns
2 teaspoons salt
3 to 4 salmon steaks
  Hollandaise Sauce (page 40)

In saucepot, combine 1½ pints water and all ingredients except salmon and Hollandaise. Simmer 30 minutes; strain into large frying pan. Wrap each salmon steak in piece of cheesecloth. Place in hot liquid. Cover. Cook over low heat until fish flakes easily, about 15 minutes. Remove cheesecloth. Serve hot or cold with Hollandaise Sauce.

Mediterranean Fish Rolls

6 servings

2 pounds fillets of sole
  Juice of ½ lemon
  Salt and pepper, divided
1 small onion, finely chopped
1 clove garlic, finely chopped
2 tablespoons vegetable oil

6 tablespoons Hunt's tomato purée
¼ teaspoon oregano
3 tablespoons dry white wine
  Lemon wedges (optional)
  Parsley (optional)

Cut fillets in half lengthwise. Sprinkle with lemon juice, salt, and pepper. Roll up and fasten with wooden cocktail sticks. Place in greased baking tin. In frying pan, fry onion and garlic in oil until onion is transparent. Add tomato purée, ½ pint water, ½ teaspoon salt, ¼ teaspoon pepper, and oregano; mix well. Simmer, uncovered, 10 minutes. Preheat oven to 190°C. (375°F.), Gas Mark 5. Add wine to sauce and pour over fish. Bake 35 minutes or until fish flakes easily. Baste occasionally. Garnish with lemon wedges and parsley.

COMPLEMENTARY SAUCES

Poached Salmon (page 37) with Hollandaise Sauce (page 40)

Hollandaise Sauce

½ pint

4 ounces butter or margarine
3 egg yolks
3 tablespoons lemon juice

¼ teaspoon salt
Pinch cayenne pepper

In small saucepot, heat fat until bubbling but not brown. Put remaining ingredients into liquidiser or food processor in order listed. Cover; process until thoroughly mixed. While blender or processor is running, add hot fat in slow, steady stream. Serve immediately or keep warm in basin over hot water.

SAUCE MOUSSELINE: Prepare Hollandaise Sauce as directed above. Beat ¼ pint double cream until stiff; fold into Hollandaise. Serve with vegetables or fish. Makes ¾ pint.

White Sauce

About ½ pint

Scant ½ pint milk
1 ounce butter or margarine,
    softened

1½ tablespoons plain flour
¼ teaspoon salt
Pinch pepper

Put all ingredients into liquidiser or food processor and process until smooth. Pour into small saucepot. Cook over moderate heat, stirring constantly, until mixture thickens and comes to the boil.

THIN WHITE SAUCE: Prepare White Sauce, using ½ ounce fat and 1 tablespoon flour.

THICK WHITE SAUCE: Prepare White Sauce, using 1½ ounces fat and 3 tablespoons plain flour.

Mustard Sauce

About ⅓ pint

2 egg yolks
3 cloves garlic, halved
¾ teaspoon salt
¼ teaspoon pepper

2 teaspoons lemon juice, divided
6½ teaspoons olive or vegetable oil,
   divided

Put egg yolks, garlic, salt, pepper, and 1 teaspoon lemon juice into liquidiser or food processor and process until garlic is very finely chopped. Slowly add half the oil and remaining lemon juice. While liquidiser is running, slowly add remaining oil. Serve with lamb, boiled beef, or fish.

Wayside Inn Mushroom Sauce

About 1½ pints

2 ounces butter or margarine
½ teaspoon salt
   Pinch pepper
5 tablespoons plain flour
¼ pint single cream

1 tin (10½ ounces) beef consommé
   or ½ pint beef or chicken stock
3 tablespoons Burgundy wine
12 large fresh mushrooms, sliced

In saucepot, melt fat and stir in salt, pepper, and flour. Stir over low heat 5 minutes, but do not brown. Stir in cream gradually until smooth. Stir in consommé, ⅓ pint water, and wine. Cook, stirring, over low heat until sauce bubbles and thickens. Add mushrooms and simmer 5 minutes, or until mushrooms are just cooked. Serve over grilled beef.

Béarnaise Sauce

About ½ pint

2 tablespoons dry white wine
2 tablespoons tarragon vinegar
2 teaspoons chervil
1 teaspoon tarragon

2 thin slices onion
4 parsley sprigs
¼ teaspoon pepper
   Hollandaise Sauce (page 40)

In small saucepot, combine wine, vinegar, chervil, tarragon, onion, parsley, and pepper. Bring to the boil; boil rapidly 3 minutes, or until reduced to about half. Prepare Hollandaise Sauce in liquidiser, slowly add hot wine mixture. Blend until thoroughly mixed. Serve with grilled meat or fish.

Pesto Sauce

About 1 pint

2 cups cut-up fresh basil leaves

2 to 3 tablespoons pine kernels (pignoli)

1 clove garlic, halved

1/2 teaspoon salt

Pinch pepper

2 ounces Parmesan cheese, grated

2 ounces Romano cheese, grated

2/3 pint olive oil

Put basil leaves, pine kernels, garlic, salt, and pepper into liquidiser or food processor. Cover; process until mixture is smooth and pastelike. Add grated cheeses; blend just until mixed. While blender or processor is running, add oil in steady stream, until sauce is consistency of creamed butter.

NOTE: Pesto Sauce is always made with fresh basil. It may be made ahead and stored, covered, in the refrigerator.

Parsley Butter

About 4 ounces

2 ounces parsley sprigs

4 ounces butter or margarine, softened

1 tablespoon single cream or milk

1/4 teaspoon salt

Put parsley in liquidiser or food processor and process until chopped. Add remaining ingredients in order listed. Cover; blend or process until thoroughly mixed. Use on grilled steak, cooked vegetables, corn on the cob, French bread.

GARLIC BUTTER: Add 1 large clove garlic, halved, with parsley sprigs. Proceed as directed above.

HERB BUTTER: Substitute 2 tablespoons fresh cut-up herb, such as chives, tarragon, or dill, or a combination of fresh herbs, or 1 teaspoon dried herbs, for parsley. Proceed as directed above.

Pesto Sauce

DELICIOUS BREADS AND COFFEE CAKES

Apricot Rum Baba (page 48),
Coconut Rolls (page 46),
Fruit-Filled Ring (page 48)

American Muffins

1 dozen

8 ounces plain flour
2½ teaspoons baking powder
½ teaspoon salt
2 tablespoons castor sugar

Scant ½ pint milk
1 egg
4 tablespoons cooking oil

Preheat oven to 200°C. (400°F.), Gas Mark 6. Grease 12 muffin tins. Sift flour, baking powder, salt, and sugar into medium-size bowl. Combine remaining ingredients in small bowl until well mixed. Pour over dry ingredients; stir until moistened. Fill muffin tins two-thirds full. Bake 20 to 25 minutes, or until done.

BLUEBERRY MUFFINS: Fold 4 ounces washed fresh blueberries into batter. Proceed as directed above.

CARROT MUFFINS: Grate 1 carrot; add to liquid ingredients. Proceed as directed above.

CRANBERRY MUFFINS: Add 4 ounces whole cranberries and 2 ounces additional castor sugar to dry ingredients. Proceed as directed above.

DATE-NUT MUFFINS: Add 4 ounces chopped stoned dates and 1 ounce chopped walnuts to dry ingredients. Proceed as directed above.

RAISIN MUFFINS: Add 4 ounces sultanas to dry ingredients. Proceed as directed above.

Coconut Rolls

2 dozen rolls

1 recipe Sweet Dough (page 51)
2 ounces butter, softened, divided
3½ ounces desiccated coconut

2 ounces sugar
½ teaspoon mace

Divide dough in half. Roll each half to 20x30-cm (8x12-inch) rectangle. Spread each with 1 ounce butter. Combine coconut, sugar, and mace and sprinkle over rectangles. Starting at 30-cm (12-inch) side, roll dough, Swiss-roll fashion. Cut into 2.5-cm (1-inch) slices. Place slices, cut-side down, in buttered deep-bun tins. Cover and let rise in warm place, free from draught, until doubled in bulk, 30 to 45 minutes. Preheat oven to 180°C. (350°F.), Gas Mark 4. Bake 20 to 30 minutes, or until done. Remove from pans immediately.

Apricot Rum Baba

1 recipe Sweet Dough (page 51)

6 tablespoons apricot jam

3 tablespoons rum

Grease 2 3/4-pint ring mould. Prepare sweet dough according to recipe directions. Preheat oven to 200°C. (400°F.), Gas Mark 6. Place dough in mold. Bake 30 minutes. (If top of cake begins to brown too much, cover with piece of aluminium foil.) In small saucepot, heat jam until warm. Stir in rum. Turn baba out of tin into shallow dish. Pour sauce over baba immediately. Continue basting with mixture until baba has absorbed all the mixture. Cool before serving.

Fruit-Filled Ring

1/2 recipe Sweet Dough (page 51)

6 ounces fruit pie filling

Icing glaze (optional)

Punch dough down. On lightly floured board, roll dough into 24x44-cm (10x16 inch) rectangle. Spread with chosen filling. Roll up from long side, Swiss-roll fashion, to form 44-cm (16-inch) roll. Pinch seam to seal. Form into ring on greased baking tray. With scissors, make cuts two-thirds of the way through ring at 2.5-cm (1-inch) intervals. Turn 1 section toward center, next toward outside of ring; continue in this fashion all the way around ring. Cover; let rise in warm place, free from draught, until doubled in bulk, about 1 hour. Preheat oven to 180°C (350°F.), Gas Mark 4. Bake about 25 minutes, or until golden brown. Remove from baking tray and cool on wire rack. Ring can be drizzled with thin icing glaze before serving.

Popovers

Scant ½ pint milk
2 eggs
1 tablespoon cooking oil

4 ounces sifted plain flour
½ teaspoon salt

Have all ingredients at room temperature. Preheat oven to 200°C. (400°F.), Gas Mark 6. Grease 8 small Yorkshire pudding tins thoroughly. Put all ingredients into liquidiser container in order listed. Cover; blend until well mixed. Fill tins. Place on baking tray. Bake 40 minutes, or until golden brown; do not open oven door while baking. Serve at once.

CHEESE POPOVERS: Place cubed Cheddar or Gruyère cheese in center of each filled Yorkshire pudding tin. Bake as directed above.

Banana-Nut Tea Bread

1 loaf

3 ounces butter or margarine
5 ounces castor sugar
2 eggs
6 ounces finely chopped walnuts
5½ ounces plain flour

2 teaspoons baking powder
¼ teaspoon bicarbonate of soda
½ teaspoon salt
2 to 3 ripe bananas, mashed

Preheat 180°C. (350°F.), Gas Mark 4. Grease a 1-pound loaf tin. Cream fat and sugar together until fluffy. Add eggs and whisk thoroughly. Add nuts and blend until smooth. Sift together flour, baking powder, bicarbonate of soda, and salt. Add sifted mixture to creamed mixture alternately with bananas, blending well after each addition. Turn batter into prepared tin. Bake 1 hour and 20 minutes, or until cake tester inserted in centre of bread comes out clean. Let stand in tin 5 minutes. Turn out on wire rack and cool thoroughly before cutting.

Sweet Dough for Coffee Cakes

Enough dough for 2 coffee cakes

6½ tablespoons milk, scalded
2½ ounces castor sugar
¼ teaspoon salt
4 ounces butter

½ ounce fresh yeast
2 eggs, well beaten
½ teaspoon almond or vanilla essence
1 to 1¼ pounds plain flour, divided

In bowl, combine hot milk, sugar, salt, and fat. Cool to lukewarm. Measure 6½ tablespoons warm water into large warm bowl. Sprinkle in yeast; stir until dissolved. Stir in lukewarm milk mixture, beaten eggs, almond or vanilla essence, and half the flour. Whisk until smooth. Stir in enough additional flour to make a slightly stiff dough. Turn out onto lightly floured board. Knead until smooth and elastic, about 8 minutes. Place in greased bowl, turning to grease top of dough. Cover; let rise in warm place, free from draught, until doubled in bulk, about 1 hour. Use this dough to make any sweet breads you wish, using desired fillings or shapes.

Strawberry Coffeetime Treat

8 to 10 servings

8 ounces butter or margarine
11 ounces castor sugar, divided
2 eggs
8 fluid ounces strawberry yogurt
8 ounces plain flour
1½ teaspoons baking powder

½ teaspoon bicarbonate of soda
1 teaspoon vanilla essence
2 ounces chopped mixed nuts
1 teaspoon ground cinnamon
1 packet (8 ounces) frozen sliced
    strawberries, thawed

Combine fat, 9 ounces sugar, and eggs in large bowl. Whisk until light and fluffy; add yogurt. Whisk until smooth. Sift flour, baking powder and bicarbonate of soda, together. Add to creamed mixture; blend well. Stir in vanilla. Preheat oven to 180°C. (350°F.), Gas Mark 4. Pile half of batter into well-buttered and floured ring mould. Mix nuts, cinnamon, and remaining 2 ounces sugar; pile over batter. Pile remaining batter over cinnamon mixture. Bake 50 to 60 minutes, or until wooden cocktail stick comes out clean. Cool on wire rack until lukewarm; turn out onto platter; top with berries.

Strawberry Coffeetime Treat

DIVINE DESSERTS

Lemon Angel Pie (page 54)

Vanilla Chiffon

¼ ounce unflavoured gelatine	2 eggs, separated
5 tablespoons castor sugar, divided	1½ teaspoons vanilla essence
¾ pint cold milk, divided	

In medium-size saucepot, combine gelatine, 2 tablespoons sugar, and ¼ pint cold milk. Let stand 1 minute. Whisk egg yolks with remaining milk; stir into gelatine mixture. Stir over low heat until gelatine is completely dissolved, about 5 minutes. Remove from heat; stir in vanilla. Chill, stirring occasionally, until mixture mounds slightly when dropped from spoon. In medium-size bowl, whisk egg whites until soft peaks form. Gradually add remaining 3 tablespoons sugar and whisk until stiff. Fold gelatine mixture into egg whites. Turn into 1½-pint jelly mould or individual serving dishes. Chill until set.

CHOCOLATE CHIFFON: Mix 1 ounce unsweetened cocoa with gelatine, sugar, and milk.

COFFEE CHIFFON: Mix 2 tablespoons instant coffee with gelatine, sugar, and milk. Substitute ½ teaspoon almond essence for vanilla essence.

LEMON CHIFFON: Substitute 2 teaspoons grated lemon zest and 2 tablespoons lemon juice for vanilla essence.

PEPPERMINT CHIFFON: Substitute ¼ teaspoon peppermint essence for vanilla essence.

Lemon Angel Pie

2 egg whites	3½ ounces castor sugar
¼ teaspoon salt	¼ pint double cream
Pinch cream of tartar	1 tin (12 ounces) lemon pie filling

Preheat oven to 150°C. (300°F.), Gas Mark 2. Lightly grease 20-cm (8-inch) flan case or deep pie plate. Whisk egg whites until foamy. Add salt and cream of tartar and whisk until stiff but not dry. Gradually add sugar and continue to whisk until mixture is glossy. Pile egg whites into pie case, shaping mixture into shape of pie plate. Bake 50 minutes. Remove from oven to cool thoroughly. The meringue case will rise as it bakes, but will fall in the centre as it cools. Whip cream until soft peaks form. Add lemon filling and whip just until mixture is smooth. Pour mixture into shell and refrigerate until serving time.

Chocolate Mousse

4 to 6 servings

6 ounces chocolate cooking chips
3 eggs, separated

1/8 teaspoon salt
2 1/2 ounces dark brown sugar

Melt chocolate chips over hot (not boiling) water; remove from heat. Add egg yolks, one at a time; whisk well after each addition. Add 3 tablespoons water; whisk until smooth. In small bowl, combine egg whites and salt; whisk until soft peaks form. Gradually add in brown sugar and whisk until stiff, glossy peaks form. Gently fold in chocolate mixture. Chill in refrigerator several hours or until ready to serve.

Caramel Custard

4 to 6 servings

3 eggs
2 egg yolks
4 1/2 ounces castor sugar, divided

1 pint milk
1 teaspoon vanilla essence

Whisk eggs and egg yolks well; stir in 1 1/2 ounces sugar, 2/3 pint milk and vanilla; set aside. Preheat oven to 180°C. (350°F.), Gas Mark 4. In small saucepot, combine remaining 3 ounces sugar and 1 1/4 teaspoons water; boil until syrup is brown and caramelized. Pour syrup into warm 20-cm (8-inch) cake tin or oven-proof glass dish, tipping it slightly to coat bottom. Pour in custard mixture; set in shallow tin of hot water. Bake 45 to 50 minutes, or until knife inserted in centre comes out clean. Chill thoroughly. Unmould to serve.

Lemon Snow

8 servings

1/4 ounce unflavoured gelatine
1/4 teaspoon salt
5 ounces sugar

6 fluid ounces lemon juice
2 egg whites
Whole fresh strawberries

In small bowl, combine gelatine, sugar, and salt. Add 1/2 pint hot water and stir until gelatine is dissolved. Add lemon juice and blend well. Chill mixture in refrigerator until slightly thickened. Place bowl in bowl of ice and water. Add unbeaten egg whites; whisk until mixture forms soft peaks. Pour into 2-pint ring mould. Chill until firm. Unmould on chilled serving plate and fill centre with whole berries.

Apricot Trifle Pie

1/4 ounce unflavoured gelatine	12 sponge fingers
3 1/2 ounces castor sugar, divided	6 ounces apricot jam
2 eggs, separated	1/2 pint double cream, whipped
Scant 1/2 pint milk	8 tinned apricot halves, well drained and
3 1/2 tablespoons dry sherry	chilled

In medium-size saucepot, mix gelatine with 1 1/2 ounces sugar. Whisk egg yolks and milk together; stir into gelatine mixture. Stir over low heat until gelatine is completely dissolved and mixture thickens slightly. Remove from heat; stir in sherry. Chill, stirring occasionally, until mixture mounds slightly when dropped from spoon. Split sponge fingers; cut pieces to stand, crust-side out, around sides of 23-cm (9-inch) pie tin. Arrange remaining pieces, crust-side down, on bottom of tin. Heat apricot jam; strain and brush over surface of sponge fingers. Reserve remaining jam. When gelatine mixture is chilled, beat egg whites until soft peaks form; gradually add remaining sugar and beat until stiff. Fold in gelatine mixture and whipped cream. Turn into prepared pie tin; chill until set. Glaze apricot halves with reserved jam. Garnish top of pie with apricot halves.

Cherries Jubilee

2 tins (15 ounces each) stoned dark sweet cherries, undrained	2 ounces castor sugar
3 thin slices lemon	4 fluid ounces brandy, warmed
1 teaspoon cornflour	Vanilla ice cream

In frying pan, combine cherries, cherry syrup, juice, and lemon slices; cook over moderate heat. Combine cornflour and 2 tablespoons cold water to make smooth paste. When cherry mixture is simmering, stir in cornflour. Cook until mixture boils and thickens slightly. Remove from heat and sprinkle sugar over cherries. Carefully pour warmed brandy over cherries. Ignite with wooden match. Pile over individual servings of ice cream.

Cherries Jubilee

American Strawberry-Topped Cupcakes

8 servings

8 ounces plain flour
1 tablespoon baking powder
1/4 teaspoon salt
4 ounces butter or margarine
4 ounces castor sugar

1 egg
6 fluid ounces milk
1 teaspoon vanilla essence
4 ounces strawberry jam

Grease 8 ovenproof custard cups. Preheat oven to 180°C. (350°F.), Gas Mark 4. Sift flour with baking powder and salt; reserve. Cream butter and sugar until light and fluffy. Add egg; whisk well. Combine milk and vanilla essence. Add to butter mixture alternately with reserved dry ingredients; whisk well after each addition. Place 2 tablespoons jam in each prepared custard cup. Spoon batter into cups, filling each about 2/3 full. Bake 25 minutes or until pick inserted in centre comes out clean. Run a sharp knife around edges of cups; invert onto serving plates. Serve warm.

Little Chocolate Cakes

About 30 cakes

4 ounces baking chocolate
3 eggs, separated
4 ounces castor sugar
2 tablespoons plain flour

3 ounces butter, softened
3 ounces plain chocolate, melted
3 tablespoons cognac

Preheat oven to 180°C. (350°F.), Gas Mark 4. Melt baking chocolate in basin over simmering water. Let cool slightly. Whisk egg yolks and combine in mixing bowl with melted chocolate, sugar, flour, and softened butter. Whisk egg whites until stiff but not dry and fold into batter. Pour batter into greased muffin tins, filling no more than 2/3 full. Bake 12 minutes. Partially cool in pans and remove to rack to cool completely. Centre of cakes will be slightly underdone when cakes are removed from oven. They will become firm as they cool. When cakes are completely cool, ice with melted plain chocolate blended with cognac.

American Strawberry-Topped Cupcakes

Fresh Strawberry Pie

1 jar (12 ounces) redcurrant jelly
1½ pounds fresh strawberries

1 23-cm (9-inch) shortcrust pastry,
baked blind
Whipped cream

Melt redcurrant jelly; add 2 tablespoons water to make glaze. Wash, hull, and drain strawberries. Place in mixing bowl and add glaze. Toss gently until strawberries are well coated. Turn into pastry case. Refrigerate until chilled thoroughly. Top with whipped cream just before serving.

Chocolate Bavarian

½ ounce unflavoured gelatine
8 ounces castor sugar, divided
¼ teaspoon salt
4 eggs, separated
¾ pint milk

12 ounces chocolate cooking chips
2 teaspoons vanilla essence
¾ pint double cream, whipped
Whipped cream (optional)
Chocolate curls (optional)

In large saucepot, combine gelatine, 4 ounces sugar, and salt. In small bowl, beat egg yolks and milk; stir into gelatine mixture. Add chocolate chips and cook over moderate heat, stirring constantly, until gelatine is dissolved (about 8 minutes). Remove from heat and stir in vanilla essence. Chill, stirring occasionally, until mixture mounds when dropped from a spoon. In small bowl, whisk egg whites until stiff but not dry. Gradually add remaining sugar, and whisk until very stiff. Fold in chilled chocolate mixture alternately with whipped cream. Turn into 3½-pint jelly mould. Chill in refrigerator until firm. Unmould onto serving platter. Garnish with whipped cream and/or chocolate curls.

Chocolate Bavarian

Tangy Lemon Cheesecake

8 to 10 servings

1 ounce unflavoured gelatine
7 ounces plus 1 tablespoon castor sugar, divided
1/4 teaspoon salt
2 eggs, separated
4 fluid ounces milk
6 ounces smooth curd cheese, beaten

2 tablespoons plus 1 teaspoon grated lemon zest, divided
2 tablespoons lemon juice
1 packet (8 ounces) digestive biscuits, crushed
1/4 teaspoon ground cinnamon
2 tablespoons butter, melted
Scant 1/2 pint heavy cream

Mix gelatine, 6 ounces sugar, and salt in basin over water. Whisk together egg yolks and milk; stir into gelatine mixture. Cook over boiling water, stirring constantly, until gelatine is dissolved and mixture is slightly thickened, about 10 minutes. Remove from heat. Mix curd cheese, 2 tablespoons lemon zest, and lemon juice. Gradually stir into gelatine mixture. Mix until blended. Chill, stirring occasionally, until mixture mounds slightly when dropped from spoon. Mix biscuit crumbs, cinnamon, 1/4 teaspoon lemon zest, remaining 1 ounce sugar, and fat; reserve as topping for cake. Whip cream. Beat egg whites until stiff but not dry; gently fold with whipped cream into cheese mixture. Pour into 20-cm (8-inch) sandwich tin and sprinkle top with crumbs. Chill until firm.

Peaches and Custard

6 to 8 servings

2/3 pint milk
3 eggs
4 tablespoons castor sugar
1 teaspoon vanilla essence
1 22- or 23-cm (8- or 9-inch) sponge cake

1 jar (12 ounces) apricot jam
2 medium-size fresh peaches, diced
Whipped cream
Fresh peach slices

In medium-size saucepot, whisk together milk and eggs. Stir in sugar. Cook over moderate heat, stirring constantly, until custard is hot and bubbly. Add vanilla and cool. Split cake in half to make 2 thin layers. Spread preserves on cut side of each layer. Cut layers into 2.5-cm (1-inch) cubes. Put half the cooled custard over cubes. Place diced peaches on top of custard. Repeat with remaining cubes and custard. Cover and refrigerate about 1 hour. Just before serving, top with whipped cream. Garnish with fresh peach slices.

GOOD IDEA: This recipe can also be made with tinned peaches. Drain a 14 1/2-ounce tin of sliced peaches, reserving syrup. Dice peaches. Proceed as above, but pour half the reserved syrup over cake cubes before adding custard.

Tangy Lemon Cheesecake

8 to 10 servings

1 ounce unflavoured gelatine
7 ounces plus 1 tablespoon castor sugar,
    divided
¼ teaspoon salt
2 eggs, separated
4 fluid ounces milk
6 ounces smooth curd cheese, beaten

2 tablespoons plus 1 teaspoon grated
    lemon zest, divided
2 tablespoons lemon juice
1 packet (8 ounces) digestive biscuits,
    crushed
¼ teaspoon ground cinnamon
2 tablespoons butter, melted
    Scant ½ pint heavy cream

Mix gelatine, 6 ounces sugar, and salt in basin over water. Whisk together egg yolks and milk; stir into gelatine mixture. Cook over boiling water, stirring constantly, until gelatine is dissolved and mixture is slightly thickened, about 10 minutes. Remove from heat. Mix curd cheese, 2 tablespoons lemon zest, and lemon juice. Gradually stir into gelatine mixture. Mix until blended. Chill, stirring occasionally, until mixture mounds slightly when dropped from spoon. Mix biscuit crumbs, cinnamon, ¼ teaspoon lemon zest, remaining 1 ounce sugar, and fat; reserve as topping for cake. Whip cream. Beat egg whites until stiff but not dry; gently fold with whipped cream into cheese mixture. Pour into 20-cm (8-inch) sandwich tin and sprinkle top with crumbs. Chill until firm.

Peaches and Custard

6 to 8 servings

⅔ pint milk
3 eggs
4 tablespoons castor sugar
1 teaspoon vanilla essence
1 22- or 23-cm (8- or 9-inch) sponge
    cake

1 jar (12 ounces) apricot jam
2 medium-size fresh peaches, diced
    Whipped cream
    Fresh peach slices

In medium-size saucepot, whisk together milk and eggs. Stir in sugar. Cook over moderate heat, stirring constantly, until custard is hot and bubbly. Add vanilla and cool. Split cake in half to make 2 thin layers. Spread preserves on cut side of each layer. Cut layers into 2.5-cm (1-inch) cubes. Put half the cooled custard over cubes. Place diced peaches on top of custard. Repeat with remaining cubes and custard. Cover and refrigerate about 1 hour. Just before serving, top with whipped cream. Garnish with fresh peach slices.

GOOD IDEA: This recipe can also be made with tinned peaches. Drain a 14½-ounce tin of sliced peaches, reserving syrup. Dice peaches. Proceed as above, but pour half the reserved syrup over cake cubes before adding custard.

Index

Acknowledgements

The publishers thank the following companies for their help and cooperation and acknowledge the sources of the following recipes and illustrations:

Antipasto Appetiser Tray (recipe and illustration):

> From *The Quick and Easy Armour Cookbook,* Copyright 1980 by Armour and Company. Used by permission.

Strawberry Coffeetime Treat (recipe and illustration):

> From *Carnation's Good-and-Easy Cookbook,* Copyright © 1970 by Carnation Company. Used by permission.

Coq au Vin (recipe and illustration), Chicken with Pea Pods (recipe and illustration), Old-Fashioned Butter-Roasted Chicken (recipe and illustration):

> From *The Money-Saver Chicken Cookbook,* Copyright © 1976 by Rutledge Books. Used by permission.

Swiss Steak, Beef Ragoût, Liver and Tomatoes:

> Reproduced courtesy of General Foods Corporation from *Cora's Country Cookbook.*

Roast Beef in a Jacket (recipe and illustration), Ham Balls in Orange Sauce (recipe and illustration), Strawberry-Topped Cupcakes (recipe and illustration):

> From *Corning's Cook's Choice,* Copyright © 1979 by Corning Glass Works and The Benjamin Company, Inc. Used by permission.

Chicken Liver Pâté, Parsley-Cheese Ball, Gazpacho (recipe and illustration), Pumpkin Soup, Veal Birds, Baked Chicken Parmesan, Chicken Curry, Old-Fashioned Pot Roast, Batter-Fried Prawns (recipe and illustration), Hollandaise Sauce, Medium White Sauce, Mustard Sauce, Béarnaise Sauce, Pesto Sauce (recipe and illustration), Parsley Butter, American Muffins (recipe and illustration), Popovers:

> From *The Complete Blender Cookbook,* Copyright © 1978 by Hamilton Beach Division Scovill, Inc. Used by permission.

Pastitsio, Moussaka, Mediterranean Fish Rolls (recipe and illustration):

> From *The Hunt's® Tomato Paste Recipe Collection,* Copyright © 1977 by Hunt-Wesson Foods, Inc.

Prawn Pâté (recipe and illustration), Vanilla Chiffon, Apricot Trifle Pie:

> From *The Knox Gelatine Cookbook,* Copyright © 1977 by Rutledge Books, Inc. and The Benjamin Company. Used by permission.

French Onion Soup:

> From *The Lea and Perrins Appetizer, Soup, Main Dish, Vegetable, and Salad Cookbook,* Copyright © 1975 by Ridge Press/Rutledge Books, The Benjamin Company, Inc., and Lea and Perrins, Inc. Used by permission.

Chocolate Bavarian (recipe and illustration), Chocolate Mousse:

> From *Tollhouse Heritage Cookbook,* Copyright © 1980 by Rutledge Books, Inc., and The Nestle Company, Inc. Used by permission.

Caramel Custard, Tangy Lemon Cheesecake:

> From *Great Cooking with Dairy Products,* Copyright © 1973 by Kraftco Corporation. Used by permission.

Fresh Strawberry Pie, Danish Pork Chops (recipe and illustration), Russian Stuffed Cabbage, Apricot Rum Baba (recipe and illustration), Coconut Rolls (recipe and illustration), Fruit-Filled Ring (recipe and illustration), Banana-Nut Tea Bread, Sweet Dough for Coffee Cakes, Lemon Angel Pie (recipe and illustration):

> From *A World of Desserts and Delicacies from Solo,* Copyright © 1976 by Sokol & Company and The Benjamin Company, Inc. Used by permission.

Sukiyaki (recipe and illustration), Lemon Snow, Cherries Jubilee (recipe and illustration), Vichyssoise:

> From *Portable Electric Cookery,* Copyright © 1970 by Sunbeam Corporation. Used by permission.

Chicken Fondue:

> From *The Smucker Cookbook,* Copyright © 1976 by The J. M. Smucker Company. Used by permission.